ROCKFORD PUBLIC LIBRARY

3 1112 022803411

W9-BIA-773

J 345.7445 LOH-HAGAN
Loh-Hagan, Virginia
Salem witch trials

WITHDRAWN

101821

SALEM WITCH TRIALS

ROCKFORD PUBLIC LIBRARY

Virginia Loh-Hagan

45TH PARALLEL PRESS

Published in the United States of America by Cherry Lake Publishing Group
Ann Arbor, Michigan
www.cherrylakepublishing.com

Reading Adviser: Marla Conn, MS, Ed., Literacy specialist, Read-Ability, Inc.
Book Designer: Melinda Millward

Photo Credits: © Hitdelight/Shutterstock.com, front cover, 1; © Solid photos/Shutterstock.com, 4; © bauhaus1000/iStock.com, 6; © Kseniya Ivashkevich/Shutterstock.com, 8; © ZU_09/iStock.com, 10, back cover; © oOhyperblaster/Shutterstock.com, 12; © donikz/Shutterstock.com, 14; © Prompilove/iStock.com, 16; © Oleg Golovnev/Shutterstock.com, 18; © Everett Collection/Shutterstock.com, 20, 24, 27; © Tinnakorn jorruang/Shutterstock.com, 22; © retroimages/iStock.com, 28

Graphic Element Credits: © Milos Djapovic/Shutterstock.com, back cover, front cover; © cajoer/Shutterstock.com, back cover, front cover, multiple interior pages; © GUSAK OLENA/Shutterstock.com, back cover, multiple interior pages; © Miloje/Shutterstock.com, front cover; © Rtstudio/Shutterstock.com, multiple interior pages; © Konstantin Nikiteev/Dreamstime.com, 29

Copyright © 2021 by Cherry Lake Publishing Group
All rights reserved. No part of this book may be reproduced or utilized
in any form or by any means without written permission from the publisher.
45TH Parallel Press is an imprint of Cherry Lake Publishing Group.

Library of Congress Cataloging-in-Publication Data

Names: Loh-Hagan, Virginia, author.
Title: Salem witch trials / by Virginia Loh-Hagan.
Description: Ann Arbor, Michigan : Cherry Lake Publishing, [2021] | Series: Surviving history | Includes index.
Identifiers: LCCN 2020030326 (print) | LCCN 2020030327 (ebook) | ISBN 9781534180291 (hardcover) | ISBN 9781534182004 (paperback) | ISBN 9781534181304 (pdf) | ISBN 9781534183018 (ebook)
Subjects: LCSH: Trials (Witchcraft)—Massachusetts—Salem—Juvenile literature. | Witchcraft—Massachusetts—Salem—History—Juvenile literature.
Classification: LCC KFM2478.8.W5 L647 2021 (print) | LCC KFM2478.8.W5 (ebook) | DDC 345.744/50288—dc23
LC record available at https://lccn.loc.gov/2020030326
LC ebook record available at https://lccn.loc.gov/2020030327

Cherry Lake Publishing Group would like to acknowledge the work of the Partnership for 21st Century Learning, a Network of Battelle for Kids. Please visit http://www.battelleforkids.org/networks/p21 for more information.

Printed in the United States of America
Corporate Graphics

TABLE OF CONTENTS

INTRODUCTION

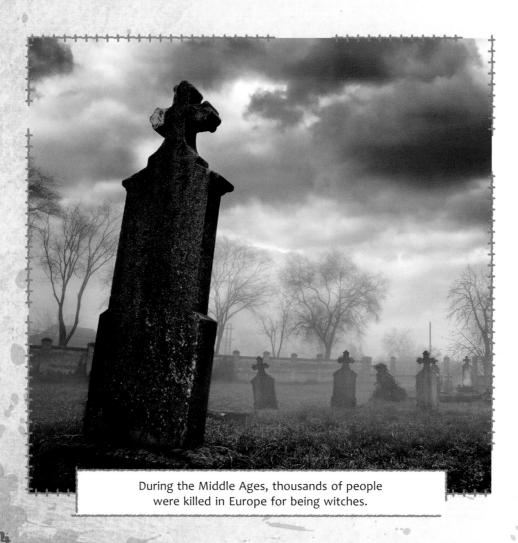

During the Middle Ages, thousands of people were killed in Europe for being witches.

Salem is in Massachusetts. It's a little north of Boston. In 1692, there were two main areas. One area was Salem Village. It was a farming area. It was on the northern edge of Salem Town. Salem Town was the other main area. It was closer to the Atlantic Coast. It was a port. It was a busy city. It was a fishing area. The two towns were **rivals**. Rivals are enemies.

In 1692, people believed in witches. They lived hard lives. They feared attacks from Native Americans. They feared **starving**. Starving is dying from hunger. Winters were cold and harsh. People were mistrustful. They were scared. They were unsure of their futures. They blamed the devil for weird things that were happening to people.

People thought the devil was causing the fighting
between Salem Village and Salem Town.

The Salem Witch **Trials** began in June 1692. Trials are formal examinations of **evidence**. Evidence is proof. Over 200 women, men, and children were accused of **witchcraft**. Witchcraft is the practice of magic. Trials were held to decide if the charges against them were true.

In 1693, William Phips was the governor. His wife was accused of being a witch. So, he ordered the arrests to stop. The Salem Witch Trials ended in May 1693.

The Salem Witch Trials were the deadliest witch hunt in U.S. history. Twenty people were **executed**. Executed means put to death. Four others died in jail while waiting for a trial.

MAN OR WOMAN?

On June 2, 1692, Bridget Bishop was the first to be tried and convicted of witchcraft. She was sentenced to death.

Betty Parris, Abigail Williams, and Ann Putnam were young girls. In 1692, they began having fits. They made weird body movements. They screamed. They threw things. They made odd sounds.

Their behavior was a mystery. Doctors said they were under a witch's spell. They accused several local women of witchcraft.

Soon, people started to panic. More young girls said they were taken over by witches. They accused more people of being witches. The accused were taken to jail. They were questioned. A special court was set up. It was called the Court of Oyer and Terminer. Oyer means to hear. Terminer means to decide.

QUESTION 1

Would you have been accused of witchcraft?

A You were a man. Men were often in charge. They made the laws. They were the jailers. They served as judges.

B You were a young girl. You could claim to be a victim of witches. This would put the blame on others.

C You were a woman. You were poor, old, or a healer. You weren't married. You didn't have children.

Women and outcasts were more likely to be accused. Outcasts were people rejected by others.

SURVIVOR BIOGRAPHY

Tituba was an **enslaved** person owned by Samuel Parris. An enslaved person is someone who is owned by another person and forced to work for free. She sailed from Barbados to Boston in 1680. She was the first woman to be accused of being a witch. She played with Betty Parris and Abigail Williams. She told their fortunes. She told them stories. The girls got sick. They accused her of being a witch. At first, Tituba denied being a witch. She was questioned for several days. To avoid death, she confessed. She was the first to do so. She said, "The devil came to me and bid me serve him." Tituba accused others. She told wild stories. She talked about evil animals. She talked about riding sticks. She talked about seeing demons. She was sent to witch jail. Later, she took back her confession. She said Samuel Parris beat her and told her what to say. Parris refused to pay her jail fees. She was released and sold to another man.

PASS OR FAIL?

The swimming test was also called trial by water.

The accused witches had to pass tests. They had to prove they weren't witches.

There was the prayer test. Accused witches had to say the Lord's Prayer. They had to say other Bible lines. They couldn't make any mistakes.

There was the swimming test. Accused witches were tied up. They were tossed into water. If they were witches, they'd float. If they weren't, they'd sink.

There was the touch test. Accused witches touched their victims. If victims reacted, then they were witches.

There were witch cakes. Witch cakes were breads mixed with the victim's pee. The cakes were fed to dogs. It was believed this would reveal the witch that cursed the victim.

QUESTION 2

Would you have passed the prayer test?

A You were educated. You were from a rich family. You were taught to read and write. You studied the Bible. You memorized several prayers.

B You could read basic words. You went to church. You listened to the preacher's **sermons**. Sermons are speeches. You knew most of the Lord's Prayer. But you didn't know every word exactly.

C You couldn't read. You couldn't write. You were poor or a slave.

European witch hunts were famous for trials by fire.

SURVIVAL BY THE NUMBERS

- About 1,500 people lived in Salem Town. About 500 people lived in Salem Village.
- There were 2 dogs that were executed in Salem. Children said the dogs gave them fits.
- On September 22, 1692, 8 people were hanged. They were accused of being witches.
- Dorothy "Dorcas" Good was the youngest accused Salem witch. She was 4 years old. She spent 8 months in witch jail.
- In 1702, the trials were declared unlawful. But it took over 250 years for Massachusetts to apologize for the deaths.
- Other people in the Massachusetts Bay Colony were accused of being witches. Witches were from about 24 different communities.
- One of the Salem girls accused 62 people of witchcraft.
- Salem was the center of the witch hunts. Andover, Massachusetts, was about 15 miles (24 kilometers) away. About 1 in 10 of the people in Andover were accused of being witches.

MARKS OR NO MARKS?

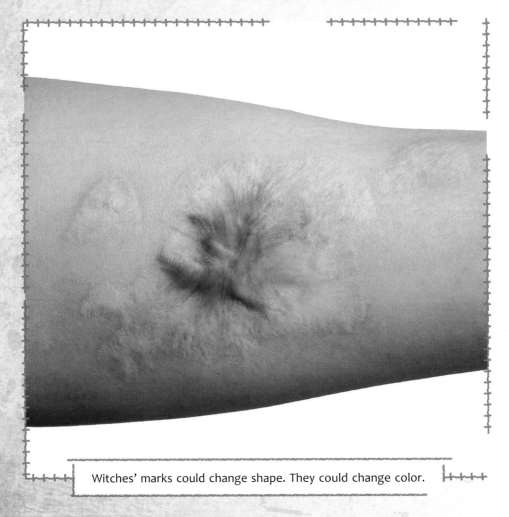

Witches' marks could change shape. They could change color.

Judges looked for evidence on human bodies. They looked for witches' marks. These marks were thought to be doors. The devil entered bodies through these marks. These marks were also proof that witches and the devil made a deal.

Accused witches had their bodies looked at in public. Judges looked for birthmarks. They looked for warts. They looked for moles. They looked for bumps. They looked for rashes. They looked for scars. They looked for freckles.

QUESTION 3

How much evidence did you have on your body?

A Your skin was smooth. You had no marks. To try to prove you were a witch, some judges would have you do a scratching test. Victims scratched you. They did this until you bled. If victims improved, then you were found guilty.

B You had a few **blemishes** on your skin. Blemishes are flaws. Judges might prick you. They had special needles. They'd poke your blemishes. If you didn't bleed, then you were a witch.

C You had a lot of blemishes. You may have tried to burn them off. Or you may have tried to cut them off. But some judges might have counted your scars as witches' marks.

People in 1692 believed in witchcraft more than science.

SURVIVAL TIPS

It was originally believed that the witchcraft victims were actually affected by spoiled rye bread. Eating it gave them a type of food poisoning. This poison causes visions and fits, which were mistaken for witchcraft. Follow these tips to survive food poisoning:

- Get lots of rest.
- Drink lots of water. Drink sports drinks. Drink broth.
- Suck on ice chips or popsicles.
- Drink ginger tea.
- Don't eat for a few hours. Let your stomach settle down. Eat when you're ready. Start with small amounts.
- Eat the BRAT diet for a while. BRAT stands for bananas, rice, applesauce, and toast.
- Call the doctor if you're sick for a long time. Call if you can't keep food or water down. Call if you're dizzy. Call if you throw up blood.
- When you notice symptoms, get medicine from doctors. Do this within 24 hours of the first signs.

FREEDOM OR JAIL?

Prisoners had to pay to be jailed. They even had to pay for their chains.

Accused witches were sent to jail. They were held there until their trials ended. The jail was a wooden building. It had two floors. It had a yard. The windows had iron bars.

The witch jail was dark. It was cold. It was wet. It had a dirt floor. It had rats. It had lice. It smelled. It was hot in the summer. It was cold in the winter.

The conditions were bad. Accused witches were treated as dangerous. They were chained to the walls. This was to stop them from flying free. It stopped them from hurting others.

QUESTION 4

How comfortable would you have been in witch jail?

A You were a man from a rich family. You could rent a room in the prison boss's house. You could go to church meetings. You could pay for a day to visit family. But you had to return at night.

B You were a woman. You were not treated well. You were abused.

C You were poor or a slave. You didn't get bedding or food. You couldn't pay your jail fees. You'd have to stay in jail until your fees were paid. Some poor prisoners died in jail.

The jail was located near the river, and the floor often flooded. Water came to the prisoners' ankles.

SURVIVAL TOOLS

Spectral evidence was allowed in the trials. Spectral means dreams and visions. People thought the devil was strong enough to attack humans with spirits. Spectral evidence should not have been considered real proof. Increase Mather lived from 1639 to 1723. He was a powerful leader in the Massachusetts Bay Colony. He was president of Harvard from 1685 to 1701. He was a reverend. He went to one witch trial. He wrote letters and journals about the trials. He believed in witches and the devil. But he preached caution. He asked people to calm down. In 1692, he wrote *Cases of Conscience Concerning Evil Spirits*. Conscience means a person's inner voice. His book was important. Mather supported the judges and trials. In fact, he praised the judges. But he rejected spectral evidence. He said it'd be better for 10 witches to go free than 1 innocent person to die. His book helped people survive the trials. It helped inspire Governor Phips to end the trials.

TO ACCUSE OR TO CONFESS?

Having arguments with neighbors in Salem was dangerous.
People accused their enemies of being witches.

Anyone could accuse anyone of being a witch. Accusing others was one way to shift blame away. By giving names, people saved themselves. But they put other people in harm's way.

Confessing was another option if you were accused. In some cases, it was the only way out. People said they were witches. Then, they begged for forgiveness. People who confessed were less likely to be killed. They were also asked to accuse others.

Confessing may have saved lives. But being a witch was a sin. People feared their souls would be sent to hell. They knew lying was a sin. They were also blamed for bad things happening.

QUESTION 5

How likely would you have been to confess?

A You were in jail. Many prisoners were abused. You had no other option. You had to confess.

B You refused to say whether you were guilty or innocent. You were tortured until you confessed.

C You were really religious. You were worried about your soul. You wanted to go to heaven. You didn't want to confess and lie. You'd rather die than send your soul to hell.

Families and friends often begged their loved ones to confess.

SURVIVAL RESULTS

The Salem Witch Trials were an example of mass hysteria. Hysteria means frenzy.

Would you have survived?

Find out! Add up your answers to the chapter questions. Did you have more **A**s, **B**s, or **C**s?

- If you had more **A**s, then you're a survivor! Congrats!

- If you had more **B**s, then you're on the edge. With some luck, you might have just made it.

- If you had more **C**s, then you wouldn't have survived.

Are you happy with your results? Did you have a tie? Sometimes fate is already decided for us. Follow the link below to our webpage. Scroll until you find the series name *Surviving History*. Click download. Print out the template. Follow the directions to create your own paper die. Read the book again. Roll the die to find your new answers. Did your fate change?

https://cherrylakepublishing.com/teaching_guides

DIGGING DEEPER: DID YOU KNOW...?

The Salem Witch Trials were terrible. Many lives were lost. Surviving history involves many different factors. Dig deeper. Consider some of the facts below.

QUESTION 1:

Would you have been accused of witchcraft?

- More women than men were accused of being witches.
- Most of the accusers were girls under 20 years old.
- Women without brothers or sons were accused of witchcraft. This was so others could take away their **inheritance**. Inheritance is money passed to family members after death.

QUESTION 2:

Would you have passed the prayer test?

- The people in Salem were very religious. Bible study was important.
- The prayer test relied on public speaking skills.
- If accused witches left out words, they were found guilty.

QUESTION 3:

How much evidence do you have on your body?

- Judges looked under eyelids. They looked under armpits.
- In England and Scotland, being a "pricker" was a job.
- The devil was thought to make marks by scratching witches with his claw.

QUESTION 4:

How comfortable would you have been in witch jail?

- Accused witches were sent to 1 of 4 jails. They were in Salem, Boston, Cambridge, and Ipswich. The Salem jail was the worst.
- Some prisoners tried to escape. If found, they were killed right away.
- Lydia Dustin spent 11 months in witch jail. She was found not guilty. But she couldn't pay her jail fees. She died in jail.

QUESTION 5:

How likely would you have been to confess?

- Some prisoners were not given water. Jailers thought thirsty people would confess more.
- Giles Corey was 81 years old. He was accused of witchcraft. He refused to say he was innocent or guilty. He was punished for this. He was crushed under rocks until he confessed. This happened for 3 days. He died.
- Witches were not allowed to be buried in consecrated grounds, like cemeteries. Consecrated means holy.

GLOSSARY

blemishes (BLEM-ish-iz) flaws
enslaved (ehn-SLAYVD) to be owned by another and forced to work for free
evidence (EV-ih-duhns) proof
executed (EK-suh-kyoot-id) put to death
inheritance (in-HER-ih-tuhns) money or property passing to family members after death

rivals (RYE-vuhlz) enemies, foes
sermons (SUR-muhnz) speeches given by religious leaders
starving (STAHR-ving) to be dying of hunger
trials (TRYE-uhlz) formal examinations of evidence
witchcraft (WICH-kraft) the practice of magic

LEARN MORE!

- Loh-Hagan, Virginia. *Witches*. Ann Arbor, MI: Cherry Lake Publishing, 2016.
- Marciniak, Kristin. *The Salem Witch Trials*. Ann Arbor, MI: Cherry Lake Publishing, 2015.
- Schanzer, Rosalyn. *Witches: The Absolutely True Tale of Disaster in Salem*. Washington, DC: National Geographic Children's Books, 2011.

INDEX

ABOUT THE AUTHOR

Dr. Virginia Loh-Hagan is an author, university professor, and former classroom teacher. She loves stories about witches and warlocks. She lives in San Diego with her very tall husband and very naughty dogs. To learn more about her, visit www.virginialoh.com.